THE LAST SHOW ON EARTH

Caitlin Press Inc.
3375 Ponderosa Way
Qualicum Beach, BC V9K 2J8
www.caitlin-press.com

Text by Vici Johnstone
Cover design by Rhonda Ganz
Edited by John Barton
Printed in Canada

Caitlin Press Inc. acknowledges financial support from the Government of
Canada and the Canada Council for the Arts, and the Province of British
Columbia through the British Columbia Arts Council and the Book Publish-
er's Tax Credit.

Library and Archives Canada Cataloguing in Publication

Title: The last show on Earth : poems / by Yvonne Blomer.

Names: Blomer, Yvonne, author.

Identifiers: Canadiana 20210314796 | ISBN 9781773860770 (softcover)
Subjects: LCGFT: Poetry.

Classification: LCC PS8553.L5657 L37 2022 | DDC C811/.6—dc23

THE LAST SHOW ON EARTH

Poems

Yvonne Blomer

CAITLIN PRESS 2022

for my son, my husband, and my dad
for their resilience and their vulnerability

A mound of refuse or the sweepings of a street,
Old kettles, old bottles, and a broken can,
Old iron, old bones, old rags...
...Now that my ladder's gone
I must lie down where all the ladders start
In the foul rag and bone shop of the heart.

—William Butler Yeats, "The Circus Animals' Desertion"

Contents

Backward We Travelled

The Last Show on Earth

Circus Moon, Circus Train

after Robert Bateman's *Circus Train - Nighthawks*

Candy-wrapper moon. Split-winged hawks. Circus train.
A dragon, silver-and-gold scaled, its lashing tail. How tent
and train drew coin from candy-flossed hands teased in by popcorn's
buttery scent. This beast once chuntered across borders. Now the moon
an opening in night where blue, grey, puce, seep in.
Here and then gone, a shadow, a species moving on a field
you see and look for again. Faithful swaying servant,
rolling, articulated, it carried animals and humans.
Mover of low moans and quick laughter,
every rail and tie a rehearsal for the last show on earth.

Waning moon. Night-stilled hawk. Broken-spined serpent.
The oiled skin and painted smiles of ballerina, clown,
strongman shine through, ghost-shapes in splintered shafts.
Light on this reptilian ride. Absence of whistle
on a field where a kid stands, frayed jeans, eyes rolled
to sky as puffed breath moves on wind. Luminous
empty moon. Feral moon. Night's coming, coming in.

Querencia

Things to chew on

after Sue Elmslie

"Each child gets cannibalised by its years."
—Denise Riley

Oh child, I would eat you up,
nibble even when I don't mean to,
as if you are a bowl of almonds
left out. I scoop, finger-stir, chew on you
with my mamma teeth.

*

Unable to latch on,
your teeth cut gums,
broke out sharp as a scream
and bit my nipple. You would not open
your mouth. Pain
a nail through my conviction. Bottle-fed-baby,
those teeth split us.

*

Never colicky. No long late walks
to get you to sleep. We were on:
stimulation schedule. Help
you get milk from the pesky bottle
(rhythmic breast-pump a sound
we all quickened to). Wake,
dance, sing, dangle toys, chewy toys,
nursing pillow merely a prop
for tummy time.

*

Diagnosis: Prader-Willi Syndrome. Key
feature: Insatiable appetite. Oh hungry
child, you've chewed the buttons off your shirt, off
your snowman, pulled threads from couch cushions,
licked the table clean. Felt pens bitten; fingers bitten. Food
hidden and still the whole of the day.

*

Were you three and a half or four? To the autism
clinic for testing. All the forms I filled in felt like
a list of parent-failures chewing through me. A second
label to stick on you. We hesitated at the door, toys on the floor
way in the distance, past all the white coats with glasses,
pens, clipboards. All of them eyeing us.
"Look how he's watching those fish on the mobile," the doc
said, as if to explain this new label. "He loves things
that dangle from string," I said, picking at its edges.
"How do you know it's not the Prader-Willi Syndrome?"
"We don't," he said, showing his teeth.

*

Which came first, the mother in me or the baby?
The worry, a stone I can't chew through,
or the joy, pollen on my skin.

*

We plan the day: 1. cuddles. 2. read books.
3. make breakfast. all the way to 15. go to bed.
Numbers are to the day as liner notes to a CD.

*

Am I writing this to you?
What will you do with it?
Feel teen-embarrassed or shrug,
raise your emphatic eyebrows,
mischievously grin, or chew
through another puzzle piece.
Tell me what number we're on,
how our days are numbered.

*

Silent soft-voiced, signing one, I begin
to dream again your speaking voice—
smooth and low—a warm hesitant hum
in the deep knowing.

*

Every part of you feels elastic,
feels glass. Wolf howl, wolf tooth,
fish scales, fish flesh. You sign *fish
taco* to the man at café MexiGo, touch
the sugared chips in a basket. *Sold!*
the man says.
I watch you fend
for yourself,
little sparrow. Menu-plan,
eat. Learn full, or fall
or fly. Say
No No No! deny
this hunger.

*

I am lying on your trampoline in the sun,
a kind of hammock. Birds dip
and sip from the garden. What will follow
when I am gone, gone?

*

Floppy. Failure to Thrive. Perseverance.
Hyperphagia. Low IQ.
High Functioning. I tell the docs,
I do not like
the language we must live in.
Shut up for a second,
quit feeding us from this
bitter jargon.

*

Fourteen now. I see new families
and wonder how we got here.
Once, your newborn foot fit in my hand.
Now, I slip your crocs on
turn the compost as a cloud
swallows the over-fed moon.

The man, watching

The woman who inserts the needle through the skin
between layers of fat, is, perhaps, the mother.

How astonishing the skin's flinch.

She presses the hormone in and waits, counts,
pulls the tip of needle out of the baby's perfect skin.

Small hand flings to the bite,
rubs to draw back the sting.
Nose nuzzles in sheets to sleep.

Closing the child's door, the woman waits, her back to the man.
He imagines her heart, a thunder in the tomb of her chest.
Its beat a shaky tenor.

Numerology

Clouds roll in across an Alberta sky. You stand in the school field. Spring.
PE. Soccer. Friday the 13th. Nothing comes of daydreams. Longing. Grass
stains on knees. Short shorts uncomfortable and the PE teacher a leech.
You live under the sky of mystery. Anything can happen. Everything can
change. Hum in your fingertips and in your brain. You walk the field, open
to whatever mystery. Goal left unguarded as light seeps in streams across the
sky. What you see is aura, the in-between, things sliding from there to here.
One girl's feet seem to lift off the ground. She throws her hands out, steadies
herself, then kicks the ball back into the field, laughing. You catch your breath
and stare, then slip home, watch for cracks in the sidewalk and in the green
screen. A dog howls. Arches his back in pain. Your mother leaves a note you
cannot read. Father searches your sister's room for clues to where she could
be. Where could she be? That shaft of light she left in. The dog's howl, a sign.
A ball arches across a field. Hits you in the face. "Get a move on," the PE
teachers snarls. Grass stains on your cheek. An owl in a distant tree. A willow
branch dipping to the earth. Your imagination hurtles back to earth. You are
an only child. The stars drain out of the night sky. Things slip in, they slip
out. Hum on skin, hairs on end. The names for things only imagined are the
names of children never seen.

Hyperphagia

Food's Child will always, always
be hungry. Vegetarian, as he grows
he will eat his mother's fingers, her face.

Can he feed the fish, the ducks or dog or will he eat their food?
His limbs are getting long, soon nothing out of reach.

At the library, Food's Child wears yellow ear defenders,
a woman stares at him, her eyes long with no loosening
smile. Food's Child is unaware, his every sense over-wrought
and something maybe edible, in the carpet, caught.

Food's Child does not talk, his tongue fears
heat, he gasps always, always when he means "help."

His father, half-eaten by remorse, never cries.
Food's Child's finger-noodles Dad's hair,
chopsticks his beard.

"No harm can come from food,"
someone once said. "Let the child decide how much."
"This too shall pass." On a walk his mother's thoughts
consume her thoughts,
this her daily (milk, salt) bread.

Sonnet for a newborn now seven

Underground we were, below the citadel,
my son, newborn, asleep on my chest.
On the streets above, Italian flowed like mother's milk
in heat. We were in a cathedral or under it. We felt
the etched walls for markings—birds or other animals.
The monks, or a priest above, began to sing. Was it *Ave Maria*
that fell through stone, through the ages and knowledge of stone?
Sound, thrum in the chest, entered us. Out of the corner of my eye
or my imagination, I saw a boy leaning in, he was my son, now.

His hands are small, perfect, though one pinky finger
a little crooked. Chords he plays while standing there, he
flicks his fingers, idle or bored
flicks and when he's lost interest, he flicks again,
taps nail to nail, he picks a low baritone song, *Gratia Plena.*

Kahului Airport

If sand or salt stitched into his fair lashes
If Kahului Airport is hot and busy
If he flings his hand out for me, does it matter his age?
If love really could break into a thousand pieces, these strands of DNA
If crying babies are a trigger and he's already on high alert
If I say no to something that pulls me away
If freckles bloom on his pale upper lip, on the skin just above
If the music is the high and low waves of Hawaiian KPOA Radio
If the airport is hot and busy and it's past bedtime late
If I could age at half his rate to be here for his forever
If there are other tired children and Kahului Airport is hot and it's way past
    bedtime late
If his movie ends
If the other children too are tired and overspent
If everyone is watching when his wall of tolerance breaks
If you take the overnight flight because it's cheaper
If the woman over there has three grown sons and two have autism
If someone said, "I have to get on the plane with that kid?"
If Kahului Airport is hot and busy and we're approaching the gate, 23:00 hours
If one finger on his right hand is a little crooked
If he sleeps in a pull-up at his age
If a woman on her cell phone mentions an earthquake at home
If I watch the woman with two autistic sons help her most autistic son
    put his socks on
If his wall breaks and his eyes show panic uncontained
If I keep an eye on his movie
If I anticipate
If his dad can still carry him and we have music and sound cancelling headphones
If everyone looks at us
If the woman with the three grown sons comes over and offers her help
If my hair retains its blonde, white-blonde shade
If the girl in our condo comes every day at four and sing-moans in the pool
If I call her a woman and not a girl

If I can draw his eyes *there,* he will see the turtle just under the tide
If the woman with two teenagers smiles as she boards the plane
If we get on last and he goes to sleep
If Kahului Airport is still hot and busy at one a.m.

First Sunset

The celestial glow of orange.
Strange light of what's forgotten lines your face.

From the ferry: peaks and blue smoke along the island's hills.
We stand, distant and blue, the ferry peaks on the hills of tide.

What if pregnant, I ask, your whiskers grey?
Or merely grey in this whiskered dusk.

The hour of distortions, refracted light.
I deflect tenderness, your hand on my hip.

Each pause from crimson to black sky, an empty house.
Each empty house a lee shore.

Sunset, you say, and sex. Dogs howl as dusk comes on.
What is natural, I say, meaning fog or low cloud on a hillside.

Smoke, you say, lit by dogs.
Dogs, I say, hackles at the door. Death, I say.

When the sun's light dies, Azimuth.
You nod, thinking, star.

I turn away.

Craning my neck from the back of the class photo

after Mary Oliver

Indignant. Loud. Spindly-legged.
The tallest kid in school, he's
underfed by his addicted-to-TV-
and-video-games-parents. Lusty.
Over-protective. Long-necked.
That goose hissing with his tongue out,
Crane is saying
"Close your mouth! Put your tongue away!"
Despair? Every day the pond fouled by rising tides and
pebbles underfoot, ducks;
"Don't piss me off," old long legs says
in his pterodactyl imitation that goose-
pimples the girls' skin. Delight:
let the world offer its imagination,
ask the Sandhill Crane
what he's doing after school.

Who sleeps here?

after Lorca

Dreams are spurs digging
into a horse's ribs. Searing
pain, a novel
full of magic, blackened
eyes, running—
The scent of rain in a time
after rain, summer fires
coming fast, horses
over the plain. Careful,
careful, careful, the poet says
but care carries a pinch
at shoulder, prick at thigh,
a swelling in joints
of a dominant hand. Sleep
is the dog, caged and turning
bumping walls and gate. The boy
who begins to speak
will never speak. Howls,
counts off the days
but to what end?
Open roads and longing
move under skin like music.
A pulse of autumn
a heart once held still. Who
sleeps here? Pinned to the wall
the unfelt earthquake
sends dust to powder face, toxin
from a toxic world. Spin
or bow to touch the ground
and the walls move. Who here
sleeps? Wander the corridors,
clear paths to exits,
obstructions moved
for the big one. Dog digs

but there is no digging through
this crate, a drum
in night's dead zone.
Such hours measured
by grief. Grief
sings its own song
full of smoke and smoke's
accompanying slur.

Lessons from my ten-year-old son

My son does not discern,
presses his nose to the sleeve
or chest of new people. Autistic
he does not shy away
or fear what looks different.
Each day I teach him
to keep his distance, raise a hand
shout in his quiet whisper, "Hi!"
but he will not. In the elevator
he presses his nose to the biker's
leathered chest and smiles. "Man,
do I stink? Cause I've been on the road."
He reaches his small hands to the springy
dark hair of a Jamaican-Canadian woman
in a café, gives her his quiet blue eyes. In pottery
class he befriends the laughing sisters with
their tight have-to-touch curls, and
in the March for Women copes beautifully
with the crowds, fingers the hijab scarf
of a Muslim woman, presses his nose
to the cool coloured silk.

Come the special-ed school bus

after Arleen Paré and the Decemberists' "This is Why We Fight"

Comes the son at the door before the school bus stops   ready to get off
comes the boy already saying something   comes home with his plan Taryn
or Turn right   comes the hop skip the sumo-stomp   comes his blue eyes
and masked-for-school face   comes the kiddo   jubilant and high strung
comes the teen   puberty coming   with pimples and hair   comes giggles
comes flinch as the wet nose of the dog comes too close   comes the sign for
iPad and "relax" snack he says   his plan for dinner comes food fixation
comes the boy finger pointing to the bus the park his life   all of us comes
boredom and worry comes his voice singing out the names of beaches
campsites   comes the song of the names of his peeps Megan Jasmine Angus
Atticus comes the boy skipping or sad swinging his backpack dropping
it for me to carry comes joy   married to chaos comes DNA   blood of mine
with a thin strand deleted   comes directions for the bus leaving us   turn
right turn right turn right   comes love   right through the door my heart
in his phalanges   daily comes the bus   comes the beep beep and the rev of
engine comes the son jubilant the bus driver laughing.

Now my mom is in a home

What is a home but this trickle of laughter?

My mom's still British
(Rhodesian) voice.

My father is clearing out the RV to sell.
Does not want help.

What is help?
Hummingbird feeder filled on a too-cold, too-bright day.

Let me do anything.

I call my dad, but I do not leave a message.
I don't want to wait for the answer machine,

which is my mother's voice from years ago,
her fluid liquid voice.

What is voice but your mother's song?

The house, I call it dad's now.
Everything used to be mom and dad and now is dad … and mom or

Where are you?
I worry late at night.

Dad calls back, "You should go to bed, I was out with your mother.
The Irish Tenors. She danced in her seat."

Mom. Mom. Mom. Am I forgetting along with her?

What is home?

The nurse helps her bathe, they have a huge tub.
She loves the sensation, warmth.

Her soft laugh, my mother-tongue song.

This here is no fine china

after Epictetus and Stoicism

"[With regard to death,] if, for example, you are fond of a specific ceramic cup,
remind yourself that it is only ceramic cups in general of which you are fond. Then
if it breaks, you will not be disturbed."
— *The Enchiridion*

Fine bone china
my mother was not, nor
was my father-in-law
a stout clay mug. The
star lily and camas come back
but are not chipped
dollar store crockery.
The last stand of Garry oak,
last Vancouver Island marmot,
or chorus of red-legged frogs
are not a set of Royal Doulton,
green or hammer white.
Nor is the Colquitz Creek,
dug up for the warzone overpass
a red Tim Horton's
disposable, roll-up-the-rim
then toss it paper cup. Everything
is dying. Elders booed at
during a political meeting
are not wooden boxes
in a museum, nor is a marbled
murrelet the lost stock of Staffordshire
enameled and gliding.

Magpie shrike

corvinella melanoleuca

Head in the shade, I am
on my back in my mother's Rhodesian garden.
koweet-koweet the wind,
footsteps on red packed road,

I am dirt along my spine.

Confusion in the cedar branches of another country—

wind-scent of earth and jacarandas—
shrike, sharp-clawed and bawling.

I am small and easily burn.

In my mother's garden the grass is never green,
in black-and-white photographs her dress stark white.

On a tricycle, perch makes bird of my spine,
hollow-boned migrant.

I am small.

No one to let the sun out, all day it yokes the house.

This, the strong one—
shrike in the bush,
at the garden's periphery and   lunch—
one sun-impaled reptile.

I am dirt and burn.

Fat in a ceramic basin:
wild black-eyed shrike.

I am two.

I am wanting.

cedar

skin

magpie   wind

This ocean is a room for the dying, Tahlequah

after Robert Bateman's Ocean Rhapsody and J35's calf

"The whales are suffering from at least three challenges: vessel noise, which interrupts their foraging; toxins, which are released into their bloodstream and calves' milk especially when the whales are hungry; and lack of food, especially Chinook salmon."
—Lynda V. Mapes, *The Seattle Times*

Tell me it is silent. Tell me it is dark
in the great undulating ocean. My mother
my mother died. She dies.

My son breaches and surfs
on the grass outside my mother's window.
Inside we bend over her.

Tell me it is still, even where movement resides. Tell me
it is cold. Speak of hunger. Of salmon
become thin.

Kelp, the whisper your body knows
it cannot feed on.

This blue light your great hall. Tell me you will surface
with your still calf for one more day. Only one more day.

I listen for your breathing, my body on the shore.
My mother dead. She is dying.

Speak of stewardship. Human words.
Calf afloat. Your blue light the gallery we gaze into.
Your strength fading.
This sea, an antechamber.

My mother breathes between my breaths.

She would have carried me. She carries me.
My son surfs in silence. Loss
a surge he could drown in.

I have never been whale watching. Would not want to be a part of that kind
of chase. On an Alaska ferry I see a pod of orcas make bubble nets to trap
herring. Stand in my own silence hoping prop and engine help confuse the
fish. An eagle, salmon in its talons, crests off the bow, flies toward land.

Surrender this body. Surrender.
Let your child go. How to let go in this anteroom.
Everyday I carry my son. My mother would carry me. Everyday
my mother's last breath.

say summer say cool tide
say chinook at high tide
say change tail thrashing
carry her carry her

Visitors pose for selfies along the city's inner harbour. This sunset something
to remember—busked music background to masts before orange sky, clouds
buoyant on invisible mountains.

Keen your water song. Your calf's
thrashing stilled. Your slow
undulation wearing you out.

the meridian moon
low tide human tide
fast coming in

Surrender breath. Surrender. You must let go.
Kelp beds. Moon jellies. Sea urchins.
Your starvation.

Tell me about your song. Tell me how long you will hold on.

How to let go. My mother breathing. Your breath.
Sing me your song.

sea otter kelp bed salt water
moon jelly sea urchin salmon
the ocean

My mother did not eat, my son would eat the world
tell me of your hunger nursing
this death.

After the eye, the butterfly

for Patrick Lane and P.K. Page

yet pale can tip the scales, make light
this heavy planet. If I were to wash
everything I own in mercury, would imagination
run rampant in that suddenly silver world—
—P.K. Page, "After Reading Albino Pheasants"

Another summer without you—
months of loss in this strange time,
while hydrangeas fade and poppies bloom
in the garden's crevices. Early mornings I listen
carefully for what moves.
Watch the rustling leaves, collisions of seeds,
fidgeting raccoons who hover over falling nub pears.
Life. So much brightness and glow
I close my eyes to thin the rays
yet pale can tip the scales, make light

a burn, rather than a balm.
We are all burning up a little
these days, you'd barely believe it.
And I'm sitting at an outdoor table
cautiously breathing, watching breath move air.
Of course, you'd have to cross some un-see-able
threshold to be here again. I miss you. The present
is an open eye; a butterfly's soft wing
caught in flight, silver pollinating
this heavy planet. If I were to wash

my hands, my face, my neck,
bathe like a posed marble statue
at an open fountain
or catch the spark that flies from earth
when the blue morpho is pulled back by gravity—

that movement of colour, only the eye
rising from page or immortal daydream can see.
Heart clamouring a bell of loss. Wash,
the world says. If I wash
everything I own in mercury, would imagination

preserve you—
I thought we'd go down differently, you know.
Thought you, the great writers, would live
through everything, like Hemingway and
Fitzgerald, distant-drinking in some villa. Survivors
of influenza and each other. Where are you?
Here, we've stepped too close to the wild, pressed
our thumb to the scaled wing, flattened everything,
swallowed the moon. And in all of it, poetry persists, your songs
run rampant in this suddenly silver world.

Creatures, already dead, come here—

One is my mother. Her smile a Siamese cat's—
her ears sharp and tail proud as she blinks a wise-eyed stare.

One is a dead poet I love. His appearance wakes me
inside the dream I'm dreaming. I panic that he has died,
but in my sleep, he lives again.

Who is here and who has gone?

The abandoned shells of crabs are numinous
and litter the beach.

                    The smallest cormorant dreams
the soft salty flesh of crab. The beach sends ominous signs to my waking self.

One is a friend who died at sixteen, our lives briefly linked.

I walk through these dreams. Are they my own?
In a mask I walk. In a hand-sewn burgundy mask.

People who have died catch this terrible cough,
die again.

Poem Without People

after C.D. Wright

Well, a great many days have passed through the garden of radishes and figs.
A fair few birds, too. Sparrows, I guess, and finches. We've not been here so
long that we can name each weed or re-attach the fallen branches. Today was
another brutal day. Death from disease. Hospital visits. The low howl of the
young hound lamenting changed plans. And tomorrow—waffles, the swal-
lowed hours. Let our breath rise and fall. We will practice slow calm living.
Well, that sounds like a balm—hand on heart, screaming. But we'll have
this paws-on-grass moment. That creeping-thyme scent. This half-overcast
thought. That butter and syrup morning. Well, I will consider reading a diffi-
cult book—*Kings* by Logue, or some such page, save the pulp for hammock
days and weekends. Wisdom falters in the wind-blown branches where birds
cannot land. The sun veiled and the day bleeding and blurring at the edges.
A toothache. A twist in the intestine. An ambulance. A man at the window
speaking in mime. The sound of a train. A cramp in the calf. A bruised banana
on a pine counter. Coffee. Cold Coffee. A squirrel hot-foots across the roof.
A great many days like this. Well, that's a list. A great many lists have been
written in the daybook of rhubarb; have been checked off in the garden of
plum trees and camas.

Bulawayo

after Natalie Shapero's "Pennsylvania"

Once, a mother, before she was, she
was a runner. The long red roads of her private flight.

I misunderstood the cost.

I thought it was love that erases
what we are. And love, a *querencia*.

Call memory, call mother. The woman, a medal
in her hand. Her coarse coat and dimpled smile—

tomorrow vanishes

the smile on her face. I yelp to run
the whole length of my one life back to her.

Of course, death comes. Then, the fuzzy
bewilderment of dreams, always

this act of endurance, but—
a hand strokes my clammy forehead,

people newly born, with her pith, born obstinate.

Pelagic cormorant

"pelagic," meaning "open sea"

The child tends to wander.
Takes his wooden dinghy, shoves off.
The mother makes him tie a line to the shore,
watches his oars lift and push,
feels a tug below her navel.
Doesn't see him catch a fish with his small net,
slice it and gut it and under his seat store it.
Doesn't see him loosen the knot,
bump the safety buoys
at the harbour's exit.

Homage

after Robert Bateman's *Homage to Ahmed*

My father on his back in shorts and hat
on African soil, is my last elephant.
He is Ahmed in that etching,
last of the great tuskers, last parent.
Wrinkles testament to both, and to the sun,
orange and wild, setting over brush and veld.
He has no tusks and no poachers hunt this man
but time and sadness do; a longing
for his younger self to surface
in a place that had entered his blood
and marrow, freckled and marked his skin, led him—
on road and curve of road,
by chance and love—to a woman, now gone
and fifty years of a life together. Elephants are dying
at the hands of men, in drought a mother
stands over a calf, dying of drought.
My father sings to praise the elephants, animals
he's come to see again and to thank
the women and men of the wildlife camps.
It is hard to go back. His friends
understand—when he lies on the ground
his whole life in that fine and granular earth.

What gets noticed

At the hospital a man praises an elderly woman, frail and in a gown, for noticing the star lilies out the window. He had not seen them, I heard him say as I hustled past with my son. My mom noticed plenty. My dad's sadness. My sister's struggles. My special son. She noticed dark shadows on my skin when I'd visit at her nursing home. Notice acne and lipstick. She said once, watching my old dog circle, "When Kirin dies, I'm going to go too. I'll go with her." Though she stayed on. Stayed long enough to meet the puppy, sometimes her hand stroking him or patting her blanket thinking it was him. These days, a year without her, my cup too full of grief, I forget to notice things. The trillium blooming in the garden. The softness of things. Forget the green of her eyes in mine. At the hospital my son's specialist discusses weight gain, puberty, iron levels, scoliosis. Does every box in his diagnosis have to be checked? Can't we skip a few side-effects, I think, having dropped him at school before heading to the dog park. The dog notices my mood, scratches at my hand for a cuddle even though I'm driving. He doesn't seem to care. Maybe I'm writing an essay here. I run the puppy round the park, well, he runs me. His excitement makes other dog walkers laugh. One lap around takes my entire life, or I'm surprised when I come to the fence that it's only my first time around. The sky above is too bright. The hours in the day—

dog wet with dog,
my feet muddied
I carry yellow pollen home on my legs.

Symbiosis above the Arctic Circle

Hum at my shoulder blade
at the back of my neck

I stand between picnic table and car,
my son flips and wiggles inside our hot tent
bright lit where the sun does not set.

hum at my left knee   near my lower back
hum by my right ear

I have stood under these low trees, washed
my hands in water pumped
from a river that runs to the Arctic, washed my dishes,
swatted at flies, told them to shoo.

hum near the top of my head   my left hand   my right foot

I have dipped my feet in water to cool,
chatted with the squirrel who ran past me lecturing,
and to the raven in the tallest of these small trees
who cracked nuts with its tongue,
gargled, clucked, watched with its black eye and its bent beak.

hum by my elbow   by my left ear   hum

A dragonfly circles me, slowly
removes each fly that has entered into busy orbit round
the gravity of my heat and sweat.
Hum   then silence   here   and here   and here
then a whoosh of air near my ear,
then nothing.

My son turns in the tent, the sun moves brightly in the midnight sky.

Horology

Water and weeds

I am the woman sitting in her back garden
contemplating drought and weeds.

When I begin to write, I want the lines of a poem
to be the small pebble that drops to the water's depths.

Sometimes, instead, a black feather
weightless and floating.

Sometimes a child's chalk candy
dissolving.

If we are happy, let it bowl us over.
If we are lost, let's find the shore.

Tonight, music and fireworks, a date,
the many years, the immigrants,
those who have come, who have stayed.
Those whose ancient ancestors wait
in the shadows of long-fallen totems,
call on the brave to again be brave.

I have been reading Thomas King and Virginia Woolf.
I have been imagining the very words and the earth they rise from,
how I too come from these places.

I have been laughing. Carefully teaching our son
how to hang laundry on the line.
Cold water, clean soap
and for a stain, the sun's light to bleach.

I am barefoot in my garden.
I am standing in the uncertain mist of history
hoping to slow the world down.

I will touch your hand,
repeat your name to remember it.

Language is alive in a poem. Memory in a word.

I am a woman standing on the shores of the great Pacific,
I am reaching out my arms, ready
to learn the first words of this land,
holding hope as I walk my feet into the jagged tide.

Pirates

The key in the ignition will start the boat. Once we can agree
on which sea and who is saddest and who will captain us—

I have a map, you a chart, edges salted.
Open wounds henceforth are your fault

as is asphalt and thunder bolts. I'll take credit
for cobalt blue and sodden poetry books, arrows and

the jewels of Pharaohs. Pirates we are,
stealing breath from birds and packing them tight

between paper wages and books on diseases
through the ages.

I have a wheelbarrow and the vessel awaits.
We'll move ourselves like goods through tunnels,

caverns of night and open seeds. The troubles
if they find us, won't make much sense—

you take the boy, I'll scramble
behind with the dog. Masked and blinded

we can swim in the deep churning sea.
Nothing will expect us, no one miss us.

Nothing can grieve this numinous gauge
that once was our grief.

Spotted owl as desire

after Robert Bateman's *Mossy Branches, Spotted Owl*

True owl. Old-growth owl. Nocturnal
owl. The clock turns by you.
Barking owl. Whistling.
Hooted notes fall from mossed trees.
Old-man moss. Knight's Plume moss. Creeping-
feather moss. Nothing human here except me.
Your eyes a lure. Shoulder-
hunched owl. Padded in your brown
mottled cloak, what are you
tracking? Fogged-in owl, muffle-
feathered owl, patience is
your domain. Bone-lichen
feathered. Lour-browed.
Old strix. What are you
making me into?

Red Bicyclette, Pinot Noir

Sometimes a little bitterness (say lemon rind) slips in/out.
What about that time, Mont Saint-Michel?
Cycled there on a tubed and taped bicycle. Fell
pregnant somewhere between yellow waves of canola
and the canal-bathing cormorant; between road
and floating abbey. Today add ginger to rocket leaves,
called something else in Canada, this peppery frond.
Mostly what you want is to live or go down screaming—
do a drop off a medieval wall, bike weightless,
maybe a red-hooded cloak floating off behind you.
Too much Disney. Too much red on your open lips.
You are sick of your yellow cycling jacket
all that retro-reflective visible from space.
Nothing gets old, not even what is tattooed in (say a
cold wind, chèvre, heart of artichoke).
1300 years of history and all you can do is sit above this vista,
the wine acidic at the edges, then swallow.

Stone, House, Straight

In a house of silence
                            night slips in.
I press my arms to my sides,
do not sleep.

On the moon
sand is burning ash.
The men in the house sleep fast.

I do not sleep, my fingers
pressed, thick stitches in
the muscles of my thighs.

In the desert a camel sighs,
lies with a loud thump, the sand
gritty and close to the skin.

Dust in light through windows,
                            dust
on the salted edge of waves.

I speak to the dog, to the yellow and black-
edged butterfly—hold my hand to its

                                        amber

wings. Mothy, the voice of silence,

                                        a breeze

over ears in the vast silence of sleep-
lessness.
                    Each breath
from the sleeping men
a drum beat that punctures skin.

The Art of Thieving

If grieving, take all you can;
(here the poem shrinks to a single silver strand)

if your dead mother visits, looms above while you sleep, try not to speak;
(a box of photos and letters, her silver chain protected on a folded card)

if silence, silence will follow;
(anyone see you slip it on? tuck it under your shirt?)

if your son keeps playing the music from her memorial, sing along;
(the rectangular pendant, the light, water, sunset, tides in glass, or—)

when her birthday comes, ride the day: Stevie Wonder's "I Just Called" to
Ladysmith Black Mambazo's "How Long";
(you will not take it off until you lose it, find it again)

if an artifact, a story;
(keep grief's ornaments safe).

Rhubarb: death in a garden

Still winter, late winter, the garnet fists push up from the heart
of the bed. Soil from desiccated house plants, the garden's ash and bone.
Daily the rain, then more rain, then a week of sun.

Fists breed fingers, loose skin wrapped at the knuckles.
Nearby a dog chases a snake into a tree's dead-end.
Sun burns the rain off and fingers become umbrellas swaying.

Hotter still, sun melts red-to-green palms open on arms now firm, purple.
In Britain, for the world-war-starved, leaves endorsed as a food source
led to a poisoned and deepening hunger. Here, I step past

the reach of these large-fanned and deadly hands. Centrepoint to my garden
they offer the only shade and shelter to this newly turned earth.
Over a day they double in size

then, pushing out from between petioles and leaves, rare inflorescences
in subtle pinks. From the kitchen I think an early squash
think a bulbous-sprung shape or what—a bird perched?

I will not harvest limbs, will not slice off their poisoned hands.
Wait to reap by candlelight their first arms,
then oats and sugar, butter, slice the bleeding limbs and bake.

Soft and tart on the tongue, and to the belly, cathartic.

Driving north to Dawson City

I'd rather be startled by, startle
a quail or ptarmigan
than a bear as we walk the Moose
Creek path but do not see a Moose.
The lady at the campsite says—
"but there's moose scat"—so contentment
close at hand. Driving the No. 2
every weathered fallen tree has antlers,
then, nearing Dawson we zip past dark lake,
I see: ungulate with nose to creek (or do I?).
It's our anniversary, we've been together
so long my gold wedding band gives my finger a rash,
so long that when we could be loving,
and laughing, we catch up on the fight we started
in the late 90s, howl like wolves (were those their footprints?).
Wife, son, husband
this trio distinct as three mountain ranges
tumbling to meet on the mosquito-festering shores
of the Stewart River.

Petit Chapeau, Cabernet Sauvignon

> "Drinking moderate amounts of wine may lead to more enjoyable sex for women"
> —facts.randomhistory.com

I'm thinking of 14 Hands and 19 Crimes. Thinking the body firm
the wine bold as cherries, clotted as blackberries.
Thinking you could trace a long finger down my spine while I trace traction:
bicycle tire on country road. Everything is sex, I'm thinking,
and it leads to a small café or a tent under a tree and an afternoon of
what? Bees. Which is just too trite, like the billow of white cotton curtains
or the dream of them. What if we spill this bottle? Redden everything?
I'm so fed up. Let's run away together like we once did
though we didn't know it at the time.
What are you thinking? Something ironic and disappointing, perhaps,
like how helicopters work. Let me tell you the blades are hard and smooth,
and they swipe at air until something happens. I'm flailing here,
throwing my arms in wide arcs hoping to fall or grip the sky.
Drink me. Put on that dark grey fedora, I'll pull my hair long.
Let's finish the bottle and eat the glasses. I want to sink into stupor and pain.
Where are you? Setting up the chess board again, while I redden
my queen, ready her.

Horology

At the train station in Nōgata
you wait.

Another train approaches,
but I am not on it.

Hours. The shorthand moves
and you wait. Years—

you will watch your mother:
the pneumonia in her chest,
in that room where time holds.

Here: men with coins for saké,
women, their kimono-pace;
pneumatic, the train's approach.

It is the cliché
of every arrival and departure platform.

But, where am I?
Is there a loss approaching—

your mother's borrowed night clothes,
your fingers at the hairline—

I am on the train now
my knee tracking its meters.

We none of us know how close the end—
        but again, the clock-sound of a train—

Northern Solstice

In an open field where dogs chase
birds and falling leaves
a woman runs her hand
along a chain-link fence, bell's song at her fingertips.
Wind claps the hands of the last leaves,
curled fingers high on a birch.
Winter's slow percussion
builds and stills.
On the scent of hush—
pant and rush of paws on frosted ground,
stomp of cold feet, chime of laughter
and low breath. Every sound rises
while the world falls away—
field sheltered under wind and the promise of snow.
Snow brings change, eases dark.
Dark will let the light in again,
voices chiming on wind.

Broadening

"Virginia Woolf's feminism, it should be emphasized, implied the broadening, not the rejection, of the domestic wisdom traditionally cultivated by women."
—Herbert Marder, *Feminism and Art: A Study of Virginia Woolf*

With something fragile balanced
on my hip, I contemplate
bed wetting and *War and Peace.*
I consider the abundance of
crumbs since the dog died, *The Iliad,*
and receive in the mail *The Paris Review.*
The washer expires off-centre so floods the basement
and my son grasps and grabs at me
wanting something beyond the few words he has,
the gestures literature hints at, the metaphors of Yeats;
wanting more than this January day; bigger than
the philosophy of Plato or Melville's whale.
Cuneiform to the lines of a Shakespearean sonnet
his desperate need, my tired arms.

Overheard conversation with self

Ugh. There is no cream.
Cream is the wise thought that gets thinned down by my phone.

Fuck the phone. The dog. What does he want anyway?
(The dog is my inner self hankering for affection.)

What am I even doing today? Obviously, there is a plan
written in a book in my not so neat hand.

If A. and I are Vancouver Island Girls,
which one of us is the bear, which one the flapper?

There is no plan. Seriously. What if
I don't live as long as I need to.

In Vernon I'd shoot off
on compass points—head for the hills above (north maybe)

or ahead (south?). I'd fast-walk for an hour. Land
at a dog park with no dog of my own so no sense of belonging.

Who belongs? My students debated this last night.
Elusive. The dogs barked at me; they knew I didn't.

What am I doing? We discussed how place roots in us, or people.
I should. I should. I should, but probably I'll just have a shower.

It's weird to meet an old neighbour in the mall and she says—
you don't actually go to a job? And I say, I work from home.

You can see she envies this even though retired. You can see she's skeptical
no matter how often I say "teach" "write" "edit"

she's picturing bonbons and, god knows, orgies. She's thinking no job.
I say—flexible for my son. She kind of half shrugs. I go and buy chocolates.

They aren't for me. This is "Yvonne," she's the "poet"—
I don't want other people's memes in my head. What's a meme anyway?

I'd ask my phone, but fuck my phone. I'll just wonder for a while.

I'm just purple-inking the page. Smoker's coughing. I'm just nail biting.
Picking at callouses. Tearing a hole in my favourite jeans.

My coffee is always cold. I'm just wood-pecking at thin treated boards.
Shedding for future bird's nests. Chewing my own arm bone.

I'm just grinding my tongue between my teeth.

The invited guest enters your psychological space

Please leave your shoes by the door
(you may wonder if some other tenant will
have moved them before you leave).

I wear a headlamp to mark a path—
picture moving streets, traps from
Indiana Jones movies I saw as a kid.

Some rooms have doors. Some
doors are locked.

(Aghast you begin
to wonder if there will be wine and why you've come.)

I am no graphic artist, but have cycled
many sunlit streets, represented in skylight
and the small cluster of butterflies on bougainvillea.

Leave the bougainvillea and jacarandas.
These two plants are my mom's.
Please don't touch. They are holding up her walls.

What more to show you?

Pardon? Ah yes
that warm glow is my husband.
My son—you can see, is light and dust and that high-

pitched giggle. You will bump into him often.
Mind the sharp corners of dog toys
and old worrisome arguments—

I beat the rugs. I vacuum. Like a giant
I have lifted this contained space
and shaken it like a tent, but such
grit remains

(yes, yes, we can open a window,
the view seems to never be the same).

I'm not sure who you are
or why you've come? I'll worry
later at blue light in the corners,

I'll worry that you took something or left
a marbled thought—crackling like static
which draws dust through crevasses,
takes your thumbprint
your measure.

Tent

from the Latin *tentus*, meaning "stretched"

Such a thin veil in which to house our sleeping selves;
all night the moon creeps in.

All night I rock my child with my restless sleep;
cocooned like a caterpillar, I begin to believe in these walls

the way in play my son forgets, leans on them.
I begin to believe they can keep things out:

ants, mosquitoes, maybe no-see-ums,
though not the campfire smoke, not a father's angry voice.

What the fuck do you fucking think you are doing!
I'm so fucking sick of this. It's midnight for fuck's sake.

His voice, his child's cries as they gravel-sling
stones inside their thin nylon cave. The conical shape of my ears.

I can plug my nose, I can close my eyes, I cannot not hear.
I sit up and shine my light out on the inner walls of this pall.

He does not stop.
You fucking got to stay up late, and this is how you act?

Other voices rise from sleep, all our tents so close
we can hear each other's soft-soled dreams.

Never sleep in the ring, I think,
circus lore on my mind this mooned night.

I think they are toward the pool, but cannot orient myself
in this shrouded space, my face pushed to my son's hair.

Like a thump in the night. When the dog lies, heavy,
a book falls or an ambulance screams,

sometimes voices of teenagers on their way home,
a woman's unsettling voice.

Once, my son woke and played his drum kit at three a.m.
Once, I made love in a tent in the middle of the afternoon.

I just want to kill myself the boy sobs out.
And then the father's voice falls to a whisper.

I listen to their sibilants; listen to the voices around me,
so close I could stroke the hair of a head, but for the thin layers between us.

I roll to my back, sit up, obscured by doubt.
Listen to the crying and the father's now softened voice.

Listen to my pulse in its own dark cloak and roll restlessly
toward sleep, my arm pulling my son close.

Labyrinth

Sun through my bathroom window makes a labyrinth
of my face as I look in the mirror

The dog shows off his ball-catching prowess, struts
a labyrinth around the grassy field that dark swallows
zig zag behind to gobble stirred insects

The Minotaur flinches
never having seen the back
of his own head

We can barely escape this classical design—
etching-like pattern the iris' labyrinth

Lab rats and mirrors
present challenges

The Humpback whale's fin
pale underwater, makes
of light a labyrinth

A double-bladed axe
my laugh lines

Unicursal fingerprints,
labyrinthine stretch marks

The house of the double-
bladed axe where the Minotaur beds down
cold and snorting

Knossos knows something
of knowledge or is that
my brain still caught in the labyrinth
of kindergarten and language

There was a king, there was a monster
We know how the powerful love walls

In sleep I take rubbings
of ancient stone buildings
labyrinth of brain and dream
history, pulse at my neck, flight and fight
I break into a sweat—
wax pastels, kohl-lined eyes

Cooking, glass of Les Vignerons

I cut directly on newly installed marble.
I do not massage the kale. Toss it in the pot with a splash of wine.
All day the rain has hammered and all day the phone: Ministry of Children
and Welfare or Island Health Authority, senior housing, a nurse,
a specialist, a doctor. The knife instantly marks the marble counter.
Its shine dulls. The dog barks and barks then wedges herself
between me and the builder. The builder has solemn eyes because a child
lost and so I love him a little and the dog knows this. Barks when he moves
from room to room. All day your father in his blue pajamas, shirt tucked in to
look more decent. The phone the dog the builder
the doctors the specialists the teacher the aide. Never
was one for believing, our son fast asleep at four p.m. on the couch
The Rise of the Guardians arguing around him. Who am I looking after?
Did you know we only have this one life and all day the rain the phone
our son's desperate grunts of need swallowed by my own and
the emails the phone the rain the dinner sizzling in its fragrant oils and
we are fine, but everyone around us and
you know I lie
         the bottle half drinking me.

Elephant in the room

In her house, built in 1892, there's a small room. In the morning, dog at her heels, she walks the passageway. The house has many rooms. It is not spacious. With its trunk an elephant can lift 350 kilograms. Nor particularly bright especially in mid-November when the rains begin. Nor warm, though when full, the house heats up. Large veins in ear flaps help elephants, particularly African bush elephants, keep cool. Her dog is whining at her feet, passing and circling back. Cloning has a 9.4% success rate for extinct species. Would you clone your mother? The tusk as living tissue has nerves all the way to the tip. Her house glows a pastel yellow in the near dark—hardwood floors, bright saffron walls, carvings of zebras, giraffes, and elephants. With its trunk an elephant can crack open a peanut shell without breaking the seed. The dog eats peanuts whole without pause. Cloned cells are inserted by a specialist into the surrogate mother of another species. The woolly mammoth-elephant clone is highly anticipated. She wonders if skin cells would be enough to pass on genes, her mother's elephant-skin purse. Called near-ungulates because they have toenails not hooves, an elephant footprint can be 1.34 metres in diameter. Her dog circles her again, his long nails clicking on the wood floors. Who can mother an elephant calf when the elephant mothers are gone? Could I, the woman wonders, slowly opening the door to the room. A fibro-elastic layer on their feet allows elephants to be very quiet. Her mother would have laughed, *such small hands* she would have said. *Such small hips.* Perhaps, she fleetingly thinks, pressing herself against a wall, a handbag cloned from her mother's laughing smile. The proboscis or trunk is a fusion of the nose and upper lip and has 150,000 muscles and no bone. It is used for sound production. In the spring her mother passed. Elephants communicate through low-frequency rumblings. They can judge distances based on pitch. The woman's arms goose bump and her armpits tingle. To survive, elephants need miles to wander, a variety of natural foods and complex family groups. The elephant has a well-developed hippocampus giving it good spatial awareness and complex emotions. The house seems to flinch when the dog barks and runs past her. The trunk is used for breathing, touching, grasping, tearing the bark off trees, removing trees to clear a path, and can wipe a tear from the eye.

How to stay married

Some might call you an old wife. Call him
an old man. You sit at the kitchen table
Manual for Marriage between you.

How *you* can be plural and singular.

Written in the 90s, it fails
to imagine how difficult eye-contact
when sun blinds from all sides:
hottest March on record, already summer fires.

The manual uses diagrams to explain simple equations:
Joint Bank Accounts, Co-signees on Mortgage,
how taxes will be interwoven:

                              Dependents.
Codependents. Bread Winners. It doesn't calculate
for the hair-like tendrils, root-like,
that interconnect unseen—

                    how you've come to share thirst,
toxins we all share, a longing for the open road... though neither of you
speaks of dreams, so hunkered in HOW THINGS ARE.

Where's the romance, captured on p. 27
in two glasses and a single rose?

Perhaps you should have gotten the manual for *Growing
Perfect Tomatoes* on the sale table
at Munro's or Helen Fielding's *Bridget Jones's Diary*.

You want to find humour in every thread,
instead, another day of sigh, eye roll, eyes on phone.

Phones are not in this manual, now twenty years old.
How to negotiate love in the flash of his
                                        Samsung Galaxy,
some British comedian and Bluetooth ear-buds?

Years on. This how-to manual
as useful as lipstick to a chronic nosebleed.

"How to Gaze Lovingly" p. 197
creates a *Quit staring at me!* outburst.

Still, he leans into you when he passes.

"Date Night" tips from p. 255
leads to an argument.
The one started in 2005 on a bike trip
in France. *Quelle surprise.*

Still, you wait for him to join you on the deck.

Pages have been torn out and argued over, paint chips
for unpainted rooms. Neither of you wonders
what the other wants,
                                        though you begin to.

Wonder is to marriage as gravity is to flight

and you begin to wonder.

The index shows a chapter on "The Long Years: Rediscovery"
but as you sip beer and wine across the pages
of this dog-eared marriage, neither of you can move—

your screws wound too tight. Still, sun-blinded,
you find each other's eyes.

It was made for you: a love poem from the future

Kiss me. Your kiss is cold bottled water on my lips.

Today the world is opening. It is closing.
A kaleidoscope of shifting
doors and windows.

Along the beach we walk, picking
our way over sharp bones
of hard plastic. Our feet printing
the sand, our voices nothing on such wind.

Last night I dreamt I was lost
in an already vanished rainforest,
and the dog, still the dog, bound
away and between falling shafts of light.

Dreams are embarrassing, but do not
be embarrassed, dreams mere
shadows and flight,
the dreamer a bird, its clawed feet
so light.

Kiss me. I'll kiss you. The last airplane full of families
flying home, this kiss. It lands and we live to cheer its landing.

Overhead: dinosaurs and pelicans. The beach
a plastic cemetery. I gather and I gather
and walk with my arms bouquet-full,
each bottle an orchid.

Kiss me. We drink water from bottles. What is clean?
What dirty? Your kiss, crystals of salt on thirsty lips.

I dream we fall through the floor of an airplane. We fall
and we fall—carbon caught in bone and flesh; bodies burn
like fuel.

I have filled a pool with what warm water I could find
and salt and shards of plastic from a broken chair,
from an ancient Coke bottle, from
thin Ziploc bags. Rest in this pool, love,
it was made for you.

Backward We Travelled

Mythology

after Robert Bateman's *Lone Raven* and the Chester Canals

Ravenous this white sky. Ravine-
watching: raw, roar, croak. Raven
is Raven's first being.

Wind grooms feathers, light washes
every surface in light. Contrast—
vole under shrub, dragonfly, tree frog—

what moves, moves with blood;
a ravening beat.

Raven pulled king Oswald's hand
from a stake, his killing site, dropped it
and there grows a spring and a tree
in present day Oswestry.

Messenger of gods in the mortal
world, no matter your truths or beliefs.

Bad luck bird, good luck bird, wise one, joker.
Ghost of murdered souls, mediator
between life and death, trickster.

Off the Welsh canal, an unkindness of—where
ducks and damselflies float, this water not
ravishing but man-made and muddied.

We do not swim here. Water raw,
never clean. We are watched by the broad-
beaked Raven's dark eye.

First intimacies

I guess he was from the Snuneymuxw Nation. I lived with my folks above
the fisheries station with a view of Protection Island and the ferries' comings
and goings. Sulphur scent of fish, scent of the Pulp and Paper Mill before
filters. The stench from the mill telling us rain was coming. We were young
and excited. We were an unlikely romance, a Saturday afternoon flick, first
love snogging in my Toyota. A friend was competing in the local pageant, so
we went to the dance together. In high heels I was taller than him. I probably
wore black. It was a phase. In dress pants, a green shirt and jacket he looked
older, but seemed younger in some ways. Worn, shy. Then, I would have
just said he was cute, dark eyes, loose in his limbs. At the dance, a seven-
teen-year-old boy I knew tried to cut in, said, "You can't dance with her." I
don't remember if we were still in High School. My boyfriend and I kept
dancing. The other boy shouted, "You f-ing Indian! You can't dance with
her!" My boyfriend stood, quiet. I was pink faced. Silent. We were under a
disco light, surrounded by all those girls in their pastel-coloured fancy dress-
es and tall boys in tuxedos. I shrunk into the floor. I held his hand. Did I look
at him? I remember we moved off. I remember looking over my shoulder,
shaking my head, a little eye roll thrown in. I can't remember what happened
next. I can't remember where we went in our fancy clothes with that sudden
vacuum of space around us. We were raw footage, discarded film cuttings
from a bad movie, lying on the ground in rain, chemical scent on the air,
inanimate and trapped in that frame.

Shifting symbols under the Big Top

Fiesta del Redentore, the end of a plague.
Canal regatta, floating bridge, lanterns, crowds in staged masks.

Of a bat, or a spider, sugared skeleton face,
children like circus characters in their vogue masks.

In a match box, in a bedside table, softly shaped
black leather, a Spanish pendant, an aged mask.

Theatrical, evocative, Carnival and Noh plays
In the shops, a queen, Jack of Hearts, a bird-beaked phage mask.

On the streets, fists raised, in a courtroom
only his eyes as he's charged, his rage mask.

We are all masked, this plague on our breath
once play, once theatre, now we are caged by masks.

Sharp on the palate this last show on earth

Breached and bruising for attention—the man, late-middle-aged, lunges—toward the curious crowd—honk of clown's horn in the distance, screech of Ferris wheel's brakes. Praise Saturday afternoon, late June, the need-a-little-excitement under the great grunge tent. The man posed—black jeans, black t-shirt—thrives on the crowd, arm extended—glimmering razor to pink-fleshed mouth—picture the salmon sliced from mouth to anus, the whale and how its body separates at the cut seem, rubber skin and thick flesh—scrapes with this sharpens, this metal in blood. How many razor blades can this clown swallow? Praise the gullet's pliability, the crowd's culpability, the flex of his trained tongue.

He swallows 5, 6, 7, each catches on the palate. Tinctured the taste of blood. The crowd squirms and he flirts. Steps back, he draws eyes forward. Then calls for a young woman—picture children taken for ransom in Nigeria, a woman held at the tip of a blade, the wolf hunted and slit—the man who has swallowed a fistful of razor blades, swallows a long piece of thread—the young woman pulls—blade by hooked blade they come out—picture a caught trout, the sea bird's gullet and gut bottle-cap full, Bic lighter full, wooden chopstick full—praise this execution crowd.

Man with a green cello case

after Chris Miles' photograph of Great Russell Street, London

A man walks with a cello on his back.
The street is deserted. Shops closed.
Let me tell you, there is nowhere
along this great human road
where a man can get a coffee to go.
Light is music as it ricochets
off eggshell blue walls,
and reflective windows. Dark contours.
A man walks. He follows
his own shadow. With each step
the cello vibrates behind him—
a death knoll, a church bell, the rap song
he favoured over Bach at age ten
before he grew into the shape, the perfect
fifths of this instrument. We are instruments
in some queer story, obscure and unbending.
Without the man, the cello looks almost human,
legless. A man walks, curves to the cello's
belly. A bow, the man is bending as he walks.
A cello floats down a street, past closed café,
closed gallery, and souvenir shop,
following a man who hums as he walks
in a minor key. His feet a thudding beat
echoing down a too quiet street.

Dinner party: Reading Odysseas Elytis

Seven people and
a candle in the white hand
of a girl—

figs dipped in red wine

The woman, her sandstone hair—
moss, moon, tin pail,
old man, monastery,
dry earth, donkey

lost in the fortune telling
lost in the fortune telling is the woman—

by evening's end
every lizard word
is slivered—

rye bread, currants, red mouths
laughter,

lost in the fortune telling
is the man—

in the ruin of wine
lost—

pear, quince jelly, red laughter,
lupine beans in olive oil

Lost in rug of bergamot blue,
in the wood floor

Lost in candles,
flicker on goat cheese, lost—

What Do You Need, What Do You Want?

Summer in the Baltics,
the sun's light flickers between showers
of thunder and rain. Sunlight
on the windowsill so you wander: brass sculpture,
mosaic fountain, baroque church. Walking
always walking through the narrow streets,
nicknamed Cat's Skull these cobbles,
also once gravestones, so Hebrew broods under feet.

> What do you need?
> What do you want?

At Kalvarju Market, red pimpled berries,
currants, pale carrots, garlic, and a sheathed vegetable,
bulbous beating heart you do not know.
On Rinkitnies Street a bright red-headed woman
in her eighties nearly runs you down, you embrace her
next time she collides with you. Now colour
rings the bells of sunlight. Summer must be almost over
in this northern land; the last gasp of heat on you.

> What do you need?
> Bright amber sun. What want.

You wander the still unpaved shtetle, between its wooden houses.
Local eyes follow as you tourist through their alleys
to student rentals, past an ashen heap. House
charred to chase the resident out (by whom?): blackened wood,
burnt kettle, ashed paper, coaled tea pot.
Your t-shirt carries the scent all day, your taste buds too
so when you dine on borscht, pink as strawberry sorbet,
it is smoked. Near Mikalojaus Street, a cluster of young women lured
by a paunchy barefoot teacher at a café table; you join for a moment
but everyone seems blinded by sun or dumb-bored;
your eyes an arbiter, glance over him, his naked feet,
and you leave.

Shiny amber pendant, dark amber pendant, heart.
At night you enter the Galaria—what want?

Arugula and a lump of mozzarella on a bamboo plate,
in a modern Italian café followed by
light and shadow through market stalls:
purple lace underwear, rusted wrenches, the bread man
winks, speaks only Polish. One of your group
translates for you and he grins, passes you a brick loaf so hearty
your arm aches—a smile for a hand; a coin for this meal.

What want? On cobbled streets each step
a pendant of thought   left step to right.

What write?—songs of stork or the songs the young sing, past twilight,
song of Vilnius stone walls and cobbled stone streets—
What sing?—overhead an airplane, thunder of rain,
your hair damp petals as you run.
How history, like choice, carries a burden.
If love: the roar of sports fans. If longing: your throat the turquoise
of sky, a bird's wing, water. What say?—each word fractured and whole—
city streets, Russian churches, choir of Lithuanians
sing from a narrow alley. Graffiti—
bear on a log. The bear of Russia.
Flags frayed.

What need? What want?
Pale amber heart.

At Paneriai your group under dark umbrellas
and Mark Strand in your head, *How lunch after Auschwitz?*
with Adorno, *Poetry after Auschwitz is barbaric,* in his.
Now sun, sights, hunger despite everything you have seen.
You begin to float above and away/toward every place and time,
history a pulsing red stone, a skull, a Hebrew word tattooed on your hand.

Warm cobbled streets,
left foot to right.   What want?

You slip into a derelict orthodox church: pock-marked walls,
damp stone, cement. Such quiet emptiness: icons gone, mosaics crumbled.
Back in daylight you pass the Gates of Dawn, to Vilnius' town hall;
street vendors on this curved lane display Gandhi, Obama, Putin matryoshka,
carved rattle snakes. A woman walks toward you, another lithe beauty;
as you pass, her bowl-belly takes shape. Startle of *Alice in Wonderland*
graffiti at the next bend, then a sign: Mint Vinetu Bookstore:
a chair, a typewriter, coffee
in the shop's lamp-lit dusk and *Frankenstein* on a poster.
An elision of vowels follows a darkening at your hairline.

What do you need?
A magazine to quiet night's sigh of want:
a title you can read; a trinket of thought.

On you walk. To the last synagogue in Vilnius, once the Jerusalem
of Lithuania. A woman, your guide, nudges you, rolls her eyes in a tease,
pats your blond strands, as if you are a child. She thinks
your surprise by tradition quaint. You nod,
yes, surprised by women still hidden to watch
the rabbi's service through a two-inch slat, hidden
in a hidden room to listen, work.
Hidden for protection, but whose?

What do you need, want?
String street names gold and white, left step to right
the vowel followed by a soft sigh of want.

You know much, you think, after days of walking.
You know nothing. Names and places slip through your thoughts—
Einstein, Freud, Chagall and the Great Gaon of Vilnius.
Somewhere, down a narrow lane, in a courtyard a statue of this

Jewish philosopher, but like so much, you
cannot fathom the where or when of things.
Milosz on the wall on Literatai Street. Words,
language shadows through the years, darken
in Cyrillic and Aleph-Bet, etched shapes
on over-plastered walls

What need. What want.
Shiny amber pendant, dark amber pendant, heart—

Your map of Lithuania, tucked, folded and refolded,
into Elytis' *The Little Mariner*, lists
jewellery, gifts and souvenirs, food and drink, barbers and
beauty. There is something you want—
some fragment of this written space—
feels like need: rooster's crow at dawn, dark alley, walk
following the River Neris, how it
divides the city.

Each step, left foot to right—
What do you need? Want?

The obscenely wealthy

after Michael Marshall, "Covid-19 a Blessing for Pangolins"
from *The Guardian*, April 18, 2020

They look like scaly anteaters—unique
among mammals, their bodies covered
in hard protective scales made of keratin;
the nails of other's fingers.

They feed, are nocturnal and often shy.
While they may look like anteaters
their closest living relatives are carnivorans:
wolves and cats. There are eight species,
all are at risk of extinction; or should be.

The idea that the obscenely wealthy
gave us Covid-19 emerged in February.
In comparing them to humans
the virus is 99% similar.
However, other scientists have yet
to study the details.

The Chinese government has lurched
into action, announcing an immediate ban
on the obscenely wealthy and any trade with them.
But, back in 2016 the international trade
with the obscenely wealthy was banned
with no drastic reduction.

More recently, China has seen a drop
in state-insurance providers announcing
they would stop covering medicines
made by or for the obscenely wealthy

hoping to ensure worldwide safety
and to better understand how the virus travelled
from them to humans. Some scientists
study links to bats, while others continue to research
the obscenely wealthy.

Occupare

from the Latin meaning, "to take possession of"

Heretics, we tore what had been made over millennia and paved over cycads, stag horn fern, horsetail. Molten lava cooled and we shaped it to our needs. A thousand-year-old tortoise pokes its head above the water in a pond in a city. An abandoned castle floats on an island in this pond. The pond is the centre of a city that has seen war, was made during war. In the tortoise, a god was found. A statue made. A story told. Then we feasted on it. Asps circled our ankles. The hinges on the doors rusted in place. We banned automatic guns but used explosives to tunnel and bridge. Watersheds faltered and failed. We travelled faster to the last butterfly tree, the last three-toed sloth and pangolin. We brought bats home, flapped their weakened wings. Made the fruit bat sleep on our down pillows and silk sheets. Yeast rises in the creases of our elbows and our knees. Music plays. We only hear the song of birds after we've turned birds into hats, and gloves of bright blue; boots feathered. The alleys we've built are long and dark. We are wretched and gleeful in our overwrought thoughts, shooting pellets like golf balls at the sun. Millions of species. Millions of deaths. Great, we occupy the space we take, we shoot, we shoot again. Snow in our nostrils and fire in our wake we eat our meals peppered with Hades' breath.

What is herd immunity?

The herd is running, immune
to sharp branches and thorns.

Cows create 15% of global greenhouse gases.
The herd ruminates on digestion.

What is immunity? Some days the internal
metronome of me: the good, the bad, immune to nothing.

I herd my son from place to place.
In another life, a sheep dog.

Did you hear the knock, knock joke?
The one about the cow? No silly, cows say moo.

Immune to climate change,
the human herd will keep eating beef.

Thinks *Epicure*'s making changes
by not adding any new red meat recipes.

We are none of us immune, anyway, to stupidity.
The child looks up to the sky, the herd's eyes follow.

What are they serving along the River Neris:
reading Ilya Kaminsky

Pear or rain-soaked river rock

Serving love   hands in lap

Serving qualms (small silver eggs)

What say you to the rain? To the river
of morning   thread of night

(serving music)
a note in a twine of song

Serving drought   war
soil not for growing   Serving

pebbles (of grief)

In the tea house   honey
rosehip   nonsense served with fried bread,
wheat beer. Locks on a lover's bridge

What are the teenage girls serving?

Puberty widens hips
despite everything watered down

All evening they cut tomatoes
torn   bruised   overripe
serve the men's soft hands

Locks; keys in the river   rain-soaked children
hunger (night-sucked stones)

I confess we ate chocolate

after Theodor W. Adorno

First, the bus driver kept getting lost and those on it began to wonder from what edge, into what ditch we would drop. Rain; let me speak of rain in the Baltic. Rain filled the narrow, pitted roads, combed the trees where branches slaughtered peace and left cracks in all our frail judgements. When we arrived at the pristine compound in the middle of the wood and rain we stood, umbrella to umbrella. We loved our guide, her Austrian accent and suit, her brown hair and meager raincoat. We were not in Austria but in the complicated village of Paneriai outside Vilnius where the Russians dug pits to hide munitions, and the Germans used them for other things. (Have I mentioned the hot coffee and rich rye bread, the currants I'd eaten that morning? How each seedy berry bled a story, grown from fields once graves?) She talked and we followed (Jews and Catholics, some with their German heritage on their faces, some from New York or other places on the earth). She led us to the edge of a pit, a sloped saucer, green with grass. She led us there to speak of numbers, of the half-starved men brought to sort through things, of the villagers who came as if to market to find new shoes and clothes. In the small museum and the rain we read everything. Like crows we pecked down to the marrow of some bitter carrion. Like wolves. We combed for (hope) the story, the Japanese official who issued visas, the music and poetry of the captives. We were wet and huddled as a group. Then each of us, alone, walked onto the bus. Silence rode us back to the city. In our wet socks and our silence, we shared shards of dark chocolate.

Washing Dishes: reading Anna Akhmatova

Sometimes, hands in warm water, I am Eastern European. Sometimes Jewish, eating potatoes and warm borscht with friends from New York. Their accents: I want them in my mouth, shaping my palate and the taste of what I see on the street.

Have you considered a quiet revolution or a hunger strike?

I often ponder water in this northern country, its freedoms fractured, winter not its only crime.

We took a bus from Vilnius to the castle town Trakai. How language gets trapped in the lint of memory, in the slaughter of time. The Russians had rebuilt the crumbling citadel. No history in the aligned walls, the perfect bricks.

Are we *like soldiers, frozen poplars in a vice*?

The blue metal sting of cold. I feel
Russian, plunging my hands into the metal sink,
human, by which I mean, ready to flee.

What is it to wash dishes?

Under the sink, a mouse nibbles at crumbs and runs from what it hears. Its small hands are mine, lifted claw-like and white from water. Somewhere the mouse will find a safe place.

What is longing? Warm hands softened by lamplight—

How to live in history

Language is the tree holding its last umber leaf,
swaying with meaning. You tread more lightly,
listen for the break that will end
a season. Music plays. Everyone in the middle
wavers: left a little, a little right. There is a feeling
in the forest that this leaf could fall,
and it is divided by such fragile veins. Has anyone eaten lunch?
Warm lentil soup and garden tomatoes are on offer and
soup is a kind of language in itself.

It is a refugee and an immigrant: language—
abandoned, lost, sunk into bone, burnt in fire, scraped
like residue, licked clean by wolves and used again. It is native
and it is mother. On wild nights it fills dark rooms like confetti,
like shadows—nothing is real, some days, nothing is false.

Language in a line of poetry wants to tell you the truth of the matter,
the way your mother may have told you—her forehead pressed to yours,
saying: *Listen, dear, listen.* And you do because
you feel like a child and language is also family.

The wind picks up and the leaf falls. Last whale, bird,
freshwater stream. Fear forms a language all its own. Power too.
They forget that part of language is listening. Listen to the raven
in the tree. It's throwing its voice: singing a frog's song
from high in the oak. Listen again.

100

Dear Victoria: a letter from a poet gone north

I wanted to write a letter of snowstorms and ice,
caribou, their elegant hoof-prance
but rain today and we snowshoed in deep slush.

On our way back to town from the hot springs,
an elk ahead on the road. We marvelled at antlers,
a branch caught making the elk larger, more fierce.

What I know of northern lights is a dream of light
in a sky so full of stars my son tries to push his hands through.
We lie on our backs on frozen ground, watch
a cloud-whale swim toward, and swallow, the moon.

Across the great Pacific high temps and warm rain blow north
while the coast is frosted and chilled by the arctic airstream going south.

On my last day, I walk through dusky morning light
buy coffee and note the city tree still lit from last night's parade.

I imagine reindeer or caribou on Victoria's city streets,
toe-stepping in their elegant fur boots through muddy puddles
toward the harbour's wrack zone, where they paw for bull kelp.

The Last Show on Earth

Fog, Grays Harbor

for Regan

We walk when the sun and earth move again,
when the long grasses bellow the horn's song.

Damp fingers stroke me,
I dip and bob, am coated in spray
by cloud and the breath of sea lions, the breath
of the deep sea skates.

Forgetting is remembering in reverse.

Along the coast, I dance and skip, I lie still,
I slip beneath waves of fog,
feathers of fog.

To desire is to forget everything.
To desire is fog, salted breath on skin,
flesh and the tides of flesh.

When I said her broken wing, I meant
turn back. I meant: the disjointed clouds.
I meant: the tide has pulled me out.

I meant: the island, all day we walked toward the island. With each step what
we remembered vanished. The motor homes and trucks, the dogs and fisher-
men. We followed the tide. It vanished.

What shadows? All day the last traces of light, stolen by the sea.

Why care, anyway?

All day I waited for the sound of the horn. I fanned the sharp grasses. I watched the ragged masts, grown from the sea, vanish, and the perfect heron shadows. I saw the fragile purple flowers, their shallow roots. Saw the carapace of skate egg and mistook it for kelp. I dipped my hand and drank from the sea; I dipped and drank fog. I drew breath, or water, into gills.

I listened for what spills
  from this tipping
  earth.

Simultaneity

after Robert Bateman's Above the Rapids - Gulls and Grizzly

Plastic has entered the salmon, the stream
and sea, the grizzly bear too and the gulls. Also

organochlorine pesticides, flame
retardants, PCBs. These toxins—

while overhead, the gulls wait to scavenge,
eagles too, from what the bear leaves.

                                       Silence

is the space silence takes in the bear—
gut lined with human rubbish. The bear on the shore,

sail boats along the coast, tankers too and cargo ships
from Rupert. Also, screech of seagulls, shrink-wrapped

cucumbers, boys wrestling on the grass outside a school,
shriek of car brakes and crows above the trees. Fish

stocks decline. The bear gets cancer. She hoards
her after-winter hunger. What fat's left, toxin-rich and nutrient-starved.

But the fog too, the gulls, the bear's huge paws,
the clear water, pebbles and boulders,

                                        nitrogen

from salmon feeding fir and cedars, shrubs too.
The bear's hunger as she notes, warily, the gulls.

The gulls as they swoop in. The bear,
deafened by birds, the birds' squawking hunger,

the salmon's silent gasping. The weight of bear, her hoarding,
the lightness of gulls, too, how one hovers

beside the bear, the weight of fog on fur, also
the salmon, the salmon getting nowhere.

Elegies for Earth

inspired by *Dancing in the Dead Sea*, Alanna Mitchell

Ghazal 1

In the middle of the end you begin to make lists. Again.
Sea stars. Coral. Bull kelp. The American avocet.

On a bicycle riding uphill among trees, lost or close to, you plot
a route to coast. Light through leaves. Morse code. That could be expressive.

Something about speed and time. Loss, or tread's rumble on road.
You tire of marring the earth. Rust caught in the scent of spring. Rot.

Somewhere, substance, a lifeform to grip. The moon evaporates with the tide.
Rain and you, thirsty for the green dark.

If the crow steals the murder weapon? If the bicycle is no longer enough?
At the top of your lungs sing ... dew on the hummingbird's wing.

Ghazal 2

So you are tired. You sing against being human on this earth.
Sing against divine purpose and Victorian ideals.

You've seen a crow fly with a hammer in its beak.
It flies to pound the sky off the world.

Or to drop it. Banish this tide of expansion.
Sea stars with their densovirus melt in your hands.

Rain holds shape before it sinks to the green foam of moss.
Fossils of sea slugs in the Himalayas. Large and coiled.

Are you tired? The thrum and crack of the road. Weary?
The ring of shot to cull the wolf. Tired.

Schoolchildren stand over a model of their city. Squeeze black grape juice
into the valleys, shake juice-crystal-pesticide over green. Make rain.

The children watch the colour wash into the rivers.
You are in the middle of your life. You count:

when you are fifty, your child will be fifteen.
Alpine spring beauty. Belief in species.

Ghazal 3

You count species. Hear a wood thrush (population down seventy percent)
or just your pulse. An anthem rings in your head, a song of triumph.

Music makes you long for the past. Is there a present?
Cretaceous period. Anthropocene. You stand on pedals to coast—

(come on, fess up, you are driving your car).

You are caught in the bars of a song. The rain. The many goodbyes.
Pink lilies under big leaf maples. Silent tree frogs. Who you are?

Science, theory, natural selection. Western grebe. Loon. Auk.
Without sea stars, mussels dominate. Without birds?

Ghazal 4

Here, sit at the table, speak of real things (of caribou and grief, of red nail polish
and blunt tankers, of microbeads and rivers that can be lit on fire).

Are you tired of being human? Tired of the signs of weakness? Yourself.
The laced-leaf foliage of thought. Bones as signs of evolution and extinction.

Tired of dinosaurs and being in the middle of your life.
Choice is appalling—to bike or drive—gestures.

Have you said all this before? Tortoise. Sea lion. Red-footed booby.
Monkeys. Mangroves. Lemurs. Where are you?

On your bike. Listen for the rufous hummingbird.
The rusty breeze. Wing and wheel. Tremor.

Ghosts: reading Sylvia Plath's "The Rabbit Catcher"

a room with no out—in a museum—
the wind trapped as breath.
Voice is a howl, a dog, its mouth an "o,"
its head tipped back.

Ghosts speak of dead animals, they speak in mirage, a pregnant
blot gently writhing. A nation rising and falling.
Children, sparrows bleeding in a lap.

All night, voices speak to me
my tongue iron-tinctured,
dry as cornmeal. I can only listen.

Into a room with nothing but floorboards,
a spider's quiet nest, these immense windows,
crumbling buildings at their base.

I walk, my feet
cold and, so misshapen, they ache.

Air breathing air. Nothing.
What is death but a removal
unlike anything.

The dog of death in my lap
her whiskers—

or a sparrow, that hollow-boned body
stilled. And a child, children
a world of fantasy
where death can come and go.

This emptiness
a constant second hand's
stuttered tic.

Au courant

after Robert Bateman's *Silent Witness - Wolf*

"Is animal painting dead? ... I am always eager to see what is "au courant" and have
found much less than meets the eye when looking for the latest thing."
— Robert Bateman, May 25, 2011

Hiding in bleak snow, a winter wolf
shaped in triangles of ear and face, by shifts
in human space. Wolf as the howling
joy of childhood. Iced lichen, luminous moss, grey
amber-eyed wolf. When did the natural world become so...
avant-garde and plastic some giant rubber duck we
bow to. Wolf as hunger, wolf as poised grace.

Follow the cement river where fish are stained
glass shapes and wolf a prisoner, forgotten,
in a small cage. Through the museum, jump
when cougar slips along dim walls
from behind trees made of concrete. Shadows here
stuffed imitations of dark. Wolf as great aunt
to the puppy at a child's feet. *Au courant*: what happens
when there is no wolf, no path through empty forest?

Something human steps off a trail and edges near;
the grey wolf steps back, her shadow whitening.

Wild Trillium

1.

Once-road, hewn by logging trucks,
now in ruin, soil and clay, rock, boulders
loosed by salal, Oregon grape, birch, pine
roots disrupt what once was packed,
the way the seasons break
a frozen river.

Rain leads to sprouting
mushrooms, ferns, moss
runs green trails, birds fly overhead
seeding and singing. Trees are needed
woodland habitants, wet forest, shade.

Crevasse, sun-dappled, one
green critter bursts
from crack and glittering dewy-
deep earth. Green, emerald-
green leaves. White on white
flower petals. Blushingly
shy, but not yet. Not until sun,
time, threads its pale ivory, rouges it.

2.

Endangered trillium, vulnerable
green rising from earth
pushing dried leaves, mold, and dirt,
through brambles, then petioles rise, armpit-soft
eye-white and in April blush of new life ruined
under everything we've built.

Paintbrush

The human finger, the eye lash, a dragonfly wing,
the day's wind moving every green branch in the garden,
the crow's cackle and its sharp eye as I water or dig,
this is the tongue of the bee.

What intelligence I have, I leave in books.
Imagine lying under a flower to see the bee's tongue
as it slips out of its palp and sheath,
lengthens to the flower's corolla,
dips fine hairs to soak up nectar.

Pollination as sex, I understand,
but this tiny tongue too is an entering,
something quenched, something

Limpet

The tide
is coming in. The tide,
and the body hooked, a suctioning foot
to a rock wall.
On the convex surface of shell,
time in textured rings,
a few chips at the edges—
perhaps a hard fall, perhaps many falls,
a whelk's drill or
where the mother broke her toe.
She is in threadbare jeans,
her heels walk on worn cuffs.
Her son holds her leg, wants to be lifted up.
What is it to be lifted up?
Once he would have tucked arms to self,
clamped, somehow, to her chest and neck.
Now, muscled, he holds firm. The tide
those arms say. The tide,
and his body hooked like a suctioning foot.
What cannot be prised off?
At the centre, the inverted nipple,
the apex
where the one-footed animal grips.
Before the tide goes out,
before the solid rock dries,
his legs, to hold, contract.

Moose

Dempster Highway, Yukon

One must wait a long time to see a moose,
have a quiet soul longing

to see, not what one hopes, but what, for a fleeting moment—
the sun's slow slip over blue, before cloud,
the cold lakes, their grassy bottoms.

I am looking into the wild places
I am searching for movement.

The road a trajectory and the bush a blur and shadow—
a wolf or moose. In the low scrub, above

the tree line, a caribou hoof, lower leg
gnawed off. Wild, this, and ordinary.

Elusive this index finger of want: oh, there,
no there…I take on the scent of animal. I take things on.

Hide. Hidden. Den. The roar of traffic, of road construction.
Antlers of plastic bottles skew-whiff in trees.

What am I hoping for?

A sign. Not all is human along this gravelled road
between trees and mountains, settlements,
overwintered deadwood, after rain.

Not a pale rock, but Grizzly—
Not the bent drainpipe in the river,
but moose or American dipper—

Call me "city girl." All I have is imagination, yearning
as we roll the road out behind us.
The lichen and shrubs, from nothing, stir
on the green, green slope
going north.

Rivers turn to Arctic
here. Creatures here seek and avoid.

I have come to believe that to see would be to understand.
Would it? To see with eye,
rather than mind. To pursue, to hike, be part,
hear what is breathing.

Press and find that tawny animal rump, that muzzle, those antlers
not the raised roots of a fallen tree, there,

look there, in the lake centre, in the shadow, antlers,
a mother and her calf. Mossy hide   stretched light.

Scarce

after Robert Bateman's *Above the River - Trumpeter Swans*

Cream-silvered river, boreal forest, two swans move against
the wind. Silence as wind, nothing imagined. Birds
rare in a scarce landscape. Rock and river and brush.

Colour muted. River sun-silvered. Swans flying not into
but out of the scene. Scarcely there, as if
we will not find them again. The wind moving

the river's surface, sun silvering it. Trees a blur
to the swans, flying. Poised to be more scarce,
a species rarely seen—swans

pull each other out of this scene. Behind them, a slope
of green trees. An open landscape,
silvered water rippled by wind, a valley,

the pant and beat of wings. The swans not
flying into, flying out of this scene.
Earth, an afterthought.

They fly as if never to be seen. Landscape:
what falls away. The curved river, slope of low trees.
The swans fight wind, necks taut,

wings not synchronized; they fly to fly off—
muted song, silvering.

Midnight, northern boreal

for JB and TL

the animal, whatever animal
a bear cub, raccoon?

a porcupine
its coat sharpened spears

in the dark brush
            past night's middle, I approach

some low scraping animal
alert along the outhouse path

whatever animal: desire

in the blood
of night, a predator—

silent in its keys of sound

shadow
incidental, hesitant, roused

animal, whatever animal

hunched, roving,
whispers

to the absent light, the forest,
fear's blurred eye

what moves, moves

Fox: Mousing

after Ashleigh Scully's photograph "Stuck In"

So the field mouse beneath
does not hear foxy feet.

So the snow, crisp on top,
remains without a printed spot.

Because with cocked ears and body tuned
to magnetic north—the fox can maroon

its prey, hum on earth's compass
to pounce—

the fox leaps, it leaps
face-first, it funnels, teeth,
paws out, tail
like a whale's, above the surf

—and the field mouse, though fast
fleet-footed, rarely gets past.

Herons move to campus during pandemic

Herons have moved to UVic campus.
They're fishing from the biology tanks
and have built nests
in the library's alcoves.

The great blues have taken up sports
around Ring Road like the militia of yore.
They amble, long legged,
across campus fields
where students once sprawled.

I hear they've taken to the sun deck
off the Grad Student Lounge and to wading,
wiggling their long toes in the ornamental pools.

One group, keen on native plants
has gone vegan; finds the aesthetic of land
and campus architecture matches
their bone structure.

Like students once did, the herons now
stand in S formations, form colonies (who is cool
and who is not) of elaborate pair-bonding
displays and ritualized greetings. Instincts revving.

At dusk, their black head plumes
and slate flight feathers
make it seem as if graduands in cap and gown
walk in stately processions.

Redhead: Aythya Americana

after the Cornell Lab of Ornithology recording of Redheaded duck, male

What can I tell you?
I've been here before

as in a bar or a bus shelter perhaps
a schoolyard   public park   or baseball game   pitches dirty

This voice is a green gasp broken by silence
My own amongst the crowd's shelter—

or in a place it resonates—
a cave perhaps or a lakefront where sound carries

an irritation
flee under feather

Probably you hope to hear sadness longing discourse
the plight of the blue billed red-headed duck

voice calling voice

This is our social order
how we figure out who is who and where

Marco you might call it Polo

You walk   your head full of the imagined world
measures each careful step
from rock to looming climb to car
(from hen to chick to sweet water reed)

Barfly

after Robert Bateman's *Long Light - Polar Bear*

Brawny one, you lean
like some bloke at the bar, nose
lifted to catch the scent
of a bearded seal breathing
a mile offshore.

Maritime bear—
your moans and chuffs blubber-
breath; padded paws hold
you to ice. Ice the hard stool
you balance on.

Air swigger, you whiff bourbon
in spilled motor oil
along the Arctic shore,
a sweetness you cannot
resist.

Styrofoam crisps, plastic Twizzlers, rust
from a car battery at the local
dump. This want could kill you,
you short-eared giant, you hunky
boar, you statue
carved from melt and salt.

What will you binge on
when winter does not come?

Light is elemental as fur,
you yellowing ice floe.
Sun will melt you.

Paws as big as snowshoes, the polar bears dance

after Eilo Elvinger's photograph "Polar pas de deux"

in *pas de deux*—we are
graceful, slow; on one leg with *attitude.*

When ice pierces padded foot
I bounce, curse, face glacier's glare

and when slush covers solid ground
I jump *cabriole,* like a goat on slick ice.

And you, cub,
a single beat behind, leap, then

reach with your paws *en pointe*
(those sharp dark nails) and rise—

the sun is low, winter cold brings
sleepy eyes—you perform *glissade*

feet in first position, raised, *relevé*
to den, you tuck to me like a roll of winter fat,

and bow, *rèvèrence,* to sleep.

In the box from the World Wildlife Fund

there is the last polar bear.
In the belly of the box, the bear's
hollow high-strung heart
rhythmed in plush down,
a stroke of a black frown
for what melts and what is dead.

The boy's blond-shod head hangs
off his bed. He sleeps and snores,
his toes curl, his fingers slacken straight.

The boy, his skin white under the lantern
of Ursa's light.

Pangolin

after Adrian Steirn's photograph "Saved by Compassion"

Everything around you speaks of love:
the green hills and overcast day,
the coming rain, the muscled gentle hand
of a human man, the burnished copper and gold
on everything. Oh scaled mammal,
oh newborn pup, oh cracked bluebird egg,
fallen beehive, oh premature pangolin—

Love is the shape of this curled tail and
love casts its gaze shy as the pangolin's bright eye.

Night Ride

The soul, a running dog,
wants the night to carry on
and the road to be smooth and clear of cars.

Men perk its ears, their loud voices and
dense walking shapes. The body wants a soft
seat and cleated pedals. The body wants the moon, hankers

for its light, glimmering off the left elbow as hands grip bars.
The moon is a guide who sticks with you
no matter your path, and let's be honest,

the moon is constant and doing its own thing.
It is a tide within you. The soul wants night
riding from quiet neighbourhood streets,

to the main drag, which at night becomes
a desire line. Standing on pedals, arcing hard around a corner
going fast—the soul, a speedometer. The soul, a hawk,

wings spread and lifting out of shoulder blades,
rising out of breath. The soul a panther
with muscled legs.

Against the wolf cull

This wolf could be my now dead dog,
my son, the bicycle I rode over 5000 km on,
it could be the dream I had last night,
the daffodils blooming in my garden.
This wolf could be my monthly cycle,
my mother now in a care home,
the garbage I put out each week.
It could be what I save of myself
each night, the house quiet,

my mouth a dark "o" of howl.

Swans in farmers' fields

for Anita

Swans are white cotton linen fallen from the line,
tufts of pillow stuffing tumbled,
bush-snagged shopping bags, early crocuses
in thick sprouting clusters.

I am driving south, imagining the losses ahead. Swans
in the pond at Somenos Marsh. One has its head low,
its feathered football-shaped rump skyward.

I am singing
old songs, replaying my dad's words as I left him, "I'll sleep
next year or the year after," my mother, his wife,
wailing her confusion   and my thoughts wander

to death. To what is dying (the ocean, say) larger than the beautiful woman
who gave me life. Swan chicks in the yard of one farmhouse
compete for seeds, windblown and fluffed up as cotton flowers

mid-summer. I am thinking of friendship (love):
laughter over wine and the deep sorrows (aging parents,
young kids) and joys of life. I am thinking

of swans, and sparrows   and all
that I miss

in the shallow woods off the Island Highway
because I am moving, driving forward.

Still Life?

after Robert Bateman's *Manor House Wren and Roses*

What is still life?   Something
a moment   before a petal or shadow   shifts

Shifts in moments   this life
a series of stills   still images

a window   wooden shutters   a curtain
sun falling through

Roses through sun's sheer curtain   light   a wren
tendrils of scent   Brushstroke
of an obsession

Mood in light on windowsill   everything
an impression of pale grey and pink   stillness

an obsession   Mine?

What emotion in a bird?   Somewhere
a centre

centre not shown   The bird chirps   wind moves petals
        something meditative   still

something living
to draw the eye   Movement   so what's left is not still

       Still   I miss the bird
  bird in shadow

In shadow the bird watches light   light glancing
made still   and still moving

Blackened Tide

April 8, 2015

Dark Pacific, English Bay's tidal
frail creatures, our gentle damp equivalent.

How long have they lived?
Only to be licked by black crude tongues.

Mortal we creatures, numen with no wisdom.
Octopus tentacles we monster, yet

pillow-soft anemones' now wear lacy blackened sleeves.
Quivering mercurial fish ride the bitumen tide.

Salt-licked feathers now tarred.
Undulations in blue varicosed filth.

What is ocean, we'll ask. What
wolf eel. What flicker-finned?

Yearn for nothing. We are down to
zero on this terminal human tide.

Sad sonnet with extra couplet

Sad simple sonnet
I do not want to write you—
scrap paper with bird scat on it.
Silence is a plucked duck and a screwed
world of stink and yellow skunk weed.
April a month to love or die doing it.
Windblown hair, tangled reeds,
mud trails, tramped voles and biting ticks:
sad all year, we are sadder yet here—
April—what hungers, what sprouts to grow
every scented thing from last year,
damp from a winter of whine and woe.
Crucified trees show beauty's hunger:
a river cut off where the dead slumber.

       Ah, but a sonnet must have a turn.
       Not to worry, everything here will burn.

Weather

Sometimes, swimming, you are also immersed in fire.
Ash coats your wet hair, and the sun has been stolen,
replaced by an orange ball shaken to glow.

Ash in your lungs as you dive and a tree falls.
"We'll be safe here," your nephew calls
as he jumps in. How fast are you aging?

Ash fills the lines on your face like stage makeup;
the dog can no longer see her feet through water
so will not come out to you. Yelps from the rocky edge.

Yodels for you to get out or because she wants to get in.
Heat escalates, smoke in your skin, in the boy's hair.
Clouds are not clouds. Air a barrier you dive through to water.

Later, you will drive south, rub soot into your now dry skin,
lick your lips pink again. Through the fast window, trees now husks
tarnish what light is left: the incandescent shoots of spring.

At the heart of the labyrinth

for Ariel

We walk the charred land.
Sky, a tarnished bowl, earth
all dirt and brown and a shadowless slope
but for one tree. What to do but walk,
tree at the centre.

We build with each footstep a spiralling labyrinth
in dust on parched ground. A slow path
by stomp and step.
Beneath our feet the tree has already sent roots,
unicursal patterns that criss-cross as a dog might
chasing a rabbit.

By the time we reach the tree, elephant
of a willow, the sun has burned off the sky.
We hold hands, press our foreheads to its massive trunk,
let the bark and base mark us but ask nothing of this tree.
Ask not for magic nor healing,
nor for clarity, nor clear tendrils of thought.

Cracked Prairie, Prairie Fire

The sun is setting. Say nothing comes of water, light

on the surface of things, knowledge.
The dog's fear, lake-centre, a canoe and ash

raining to grey her fur.
Tremor in the hind legs, this knowing.

Speak beauty. Speak crayfish. Water in the lungs
and the lungs cannot breathe

Toothache. Say loss. Our mothers:
matrons and we are small under their giant skirts.

The sun never sets. All night we bake and breathe its light.
Speak sorrow. Speak remorse. Always humans

on their horses. Come the horses, come tractors, come SUVS galloping
through life on earth.

Tell me we won't take the last train through the last show
never stopping. Hunger is a game in this house. Speech is.

Grief a boy now man. Loss a mother not holding, not holding on.
Say hydrangea, Say dead crabs. Silent as a crow

dropping its voice, a marble down a tube, an acorn un-sown.
The last train pulls away full of fallow beings: elephant, tiger

lion, not an ending but the last refugium.

Backward we travelled to reclaim the day

a line from Sylvia Plath's "The Doom of the Exiles"

Backward we travelled
from birds nesting and laundry hung
to winter's long nights and dark
until we were reclaimed by the day.

Do not linger too long in the shower.
Do not worry. The woodpecker bangs on tin
to call its mate.

When the morning sun blinds, claim it
as your own embracing light.

Listen as the crows squawk like the siblings
your son does not have.

Winter has its ceremonies,
spring its births and deaths.

Backward we travelled to footpaths
and horse-drawn carts. We travelled, blamed
no one this reversal, reclaimed
the clear waters and quiet skies.

In this new exile we deemed hydro
and solar power, batteries and medicines
essential. Travelled from night
into day, night into day
backwards, the way
the dead might.

Stillness: year's end

after Mats Anderson's photograph "Winter Pause"

Even the snow stills
as colour fades, thins to silver
whispered in frost.   Movement
is movement held. Motion is breath
as the small squirrel stands—
wind and dust and shadow—closes its eyes.
Its small necktie of white,
its eyes lined in moon and rime,
paws held, hold still.
It twitches neither in nose nor whisker,
lets breeze on rose-tipped ears flutter,
lets sound travel on the steps of light.
Hold still. The year turns.
Its turning is this quiet.

Our one blue bowl

Praise this broken world, the blue within it.
The water, orca, salmon, seaweed, and wrack,
the crow and gull, the chip bag and butt, the boat debris.

Praise the girl for fast dip-in, the boy for skipped stone.
Praise beer cans, corks, broken buoys and rope made from hemp.
Praise fisherfolk and world trade for tankers, tugs and smoke.

This tidal, arched, foaming blue bowl.
This salted, sculpted, cracked blue bowl.

Savour what's moored by rope and net and hunger;
tied by hunger, heat and death. We taste

this grief, our marbled blue world.

Reading Rilke on my son's fifteenth birthday

with lines from "The Ninth Elegy"

For my son's sixth birthday, a friend carved
a watermelon into a cake shape.
Why, if this interval of being can be spent
remembering, am I wasting it again
wondering what bird outside is calling
and for whom? Also, the dog's deep sighs,
their meaning.
why then/ have to be human—and, escaping from fate,
keep longing for fate?
Fate, the car swerves at the last—
or before—the last moment,
the bird sees the glass and stops
before body reaches it. Always
fate stops death or attention
does—I thought, years ago (though
truly it feels like minutes) if I paid attention
the years wouldn't just fall away—
an image—I'm on a treadmill holding the baby
of him. *But because* truly *being here*
is so much; because everything here
apparently needs us—
that need is such a mothering thought.
Is it? To be needed is to be loved. Is it?
From birth we encourage each child to move away—
crawl or walk or run or drive. "Soon his driver's licence,"
said the special-ed bus driver, knowing
this will not be his fate.
Fate as in destiny. What is yours?
You ask yourself again—Rilke
offering need and the rhythm of his line.
He doesn't have an answer, but what a thinker he is.
Perhaps we are here *in order to say: house*
bridge, fountain, gate, pitcher, fruit-tree, window—
Yes, I think, and to love, which he speaks of,

that near unnameable force that is not gravity but which
hurts and holds us. Perhaps to know body,
bone and bowel. To let the pimples come and let the frown lines
deepen and the jowls of age come. To let the body rise in breath,
to suffer each bruise and cut, each terrible death.
But wait, it's my son's birthday, do not bring death here.
Bring longevity, bring life expectancy, bring life.
And now, I am eager to leave the poem, to find an exit—
how Rilke held himself in it, moved to the next thought
and sound—traffic's bleary hum on Quadra Street,
the same bird's persistent squeak, answered
from another tree. The next fleeting thought—*that
inside their boundless emotion all things may shudder with joy?*
Praise, he says, praise this—
the blue eyes, the dimpled smile, the crooked spine,
the swayed back, the loud laugh, the voice finding itself,
the unhappy yelp, the anxiety, its trilling body shake,
the curl of ear, the soft skin, the newborn, and the man within,
the resilience of the boy, the boy, the boy,
and his father, and his mother, and all—

Notes

"Querencia" is a Spanish word meaning "a place where one feels safe, a place from which one's strength of character is drawn; a place where one feels at home." Also from "querer" which means "to desire." Also, an "area in the arena taken by the bull for a defensive stand in a bullfight." All may apply.

"Things to chew on" was inspired by Denise Riley's long poem "A Part Song" about her son's death.

I read "Water and weeds" on Canada Day in 2015 as part of my duties as the City of Victoria's poet laureate. Stephen Harper was in government; scientists were being silenced; Indigenous people and settler Canadians watched the closing event of the Truth and Reconciliation Commission and learned of its findings on residential schools and colonialism of the lands known as "Canada." I was very torn having accepted the invitation to read a poem on Canada Day. This is the poem I wrote. When I read it, I began by saying, "When I sing 'We stand on guard for thee,' I want it to mean that, from this day forward, 'We stand for the first people and their rights, we stand for the natural world.'"

There are three poems about wine in this book. In "Petit chapeau, Cabernet Sauvignon," I mention two wines: 14 Hands and 19 Crimes.

"Rhubarb: Death in the Garden" is after Seamus Heaney's poem "Blackberry-Picking."

"Labyrinth" is inspired by Colum McCann's line, "It only takes two facing mirrors to make a labyrinth" from *Apeirogon: A Novel*, Penguin-Random House, 2021.

"The Obscenely Wealthy" is based on and borrows lines from Michael Marshall's article, "Covid-19 a Blessing for Pangolins," *The Guardian*, April 18, 2020. I've replaced the word "pangolin" with the phrase "the obscenely wealthy."

"I confess we ate chocolate" comes out of my Summer Literacy Seminar residency in Vilnius, Lithuania, in July/August of 2012. I wrote the poem with Theodor W. Adorno's idea that "to write poetry after Auschwitz is barbaric," which is a short clip of a statement taken from a much longer essay where he talks about the inadequacy of art to respond to actions and events in the world. This is a terrible oversimplification. Look at this blog post for a fuller discussion, go to http://mindfulpleasures.blogspot.com/2011/03/poetry-after-auschwitz-what-adorno.html, or read Adorno's essay "Cultural Criticism and Society." The poet Mark Strand responded to Adorno by saying, "How can one eat lunch after Auschwitz."

"Washing Dishes: Reading Anna Akhmatova" has the line "like soldiers, frozen poplars in a vice" which is taken from Akhmatova's poem "For Osip Mandelstam." It was on the shortlist, or a Commended poem in the 2020 Troubadour International Poetry Prize.

I wrote "How to Live in History" for City of Victoria mayor Lisa Helps near the end of the 2018 municipal election, which had become polarized, and she asked me to write a poem. After the vote, I was honoured to read it at the inaugural city-council meeting on November 1, 2018.

In "Fox: Mousing," to "mouse" means "to hunt mice by bounding on them from above."

Acknowledgements

All poems after Robert Bateman's paintings first appeared in *Ravine, Mouse, a Bird's Beak*, (Nose in Book Publishing, 2018) and in an art show of the same name, which I curated at The Bateman Gallery in 2018, with thanks to The Bateman Centre, Robert Bateman and his assistants, and publisher Linda Crosfield. Thank you also to The Good Foundation for supporting *Ravine, Mouse, A Bird's Beak*.

The epigraph with *"Au courant"* comes from "State of Wildlife Art" by Robert Bateman found at collections.batemanfoundation.org/artist/state-wildlife-art."

All poems based on photographs of animals are after the Royal British Columbia Museum's *National Geographic* Wildlife Photograph of the Year Exhibition in 2017. I wrote these poems as poet laureate for the RBCM's New Year's Eve celebration and read them to musical accompaniment performed by Cam Culham. With thanks to staff at the RBCM and a huge thanks to Cam, who got me singing like Elvis (and for his years visiting schools to sing with special-ed kids).

Poems set in Vilnius were written during a Summer Literacy Seminar in Lithuania in 2012, with thanks to the British Columbia Arts Council, which funded my travel and accommodation. Thanks to Mikhail Iossil, the director of SLS, and the staff and other students in residence with me. Thanks especially to Liz Edelglass and Barbara Tramonte. Thank you, Ilya Kaminski.

Some of the poems here were written at retreats run by the late Patrick Lane. When I reread them, I can see him, hear his voice, his hand moving as he notes the stresses in the lines. Thank you, Patrick.

Huge thanks to the editors, staff, and publishers at the magazines and journals where poems in this collection have previously appeared: *The Goose* ("Symbiosis above the Arctic Circle," "Weather," "Paws as big as snowshoes, the polar bears dance," "Overheard Conversation with Self," "Sad Sonnet with Extra Couplet," and *"Occupare"*), *The Malahat Review* ("Craning my neck from the back of the class photo" and "Rhubarb: Death in the Garden"), *The Northern Review* ("Moose: Dempster Highway, Yukon," and "Mid-night, Northern Boreal"), *Understory Magazine* ("Creatures, already dead, come here").

Poems also appear in the following anthologies and chapbooks:

"Sonnet for a newborn now seven" and "Pelagic Cormorant" in *Alongside We Travel: Contemporary Poets on Autism*, edited by Sean Thomas Daugherty, NYQ Books, 2019.

"Our One Blue Bowl," my legacy poem for the City of Victoria, is part of an art installation at Clover Point in Victoria, BC. It appears in *For the Love of Orcas*, edited by Andrew Shattuck McBride and Jill McCabe Johnson, Wandering Aengus Press, 2019, and was nominated for a 2019 Pushcart Prize.

"Paintbrush" in *Elegies for Earth* and was part of the Poems for Pollinators project with Border Free Bees and chosen by Nancy Holmes in 2016 and can be found at UBC's Eco Art Incubator webpage.

"Against the Wolf Cull," "Pelagic Cormorant," "Elegies for Earth" also appear in *Elegies for Earth*, Leaf Press, 2017.

"After the Eye, the Butterfly" is forthcoming in *Hologram: Homage to P.K. Page*, co-edited by Yvonne Blomer and D.C. Reid.

"First Sunset" and "In the box from the World Wildlife Fund" in *Make it True: Poetry from Cascadia*, edited by Paul Nelson, Leaf Press, 2015.

"What gets noticed" was longlisted for the Montreal Poetry Prize in 2020 and appears in *The Montreal Poetry Prize Anthology 2020*, Signal Editions, 2021. "I confess we ate chocolate" was longlisted in 2013 and also appears in the essay "What are you most afraid of," published in *This Place a Stranger: Canadian Women Travelling Alone*, edited by Vici Johnstone, Caitlin Press, 2015.

"Hyperphagia" was published in *Sustenance: Writers from BC and Beyond on the Subject of Food*, edited by Rachel Rose, Anvil Press, 2017.

"At the heart of the labyrinth" in *Worth More Standing*, edited by Christine Lowther, Caitlin Press, 2022.

Many of these poems were written and read between 2015 and 2018 while I was the City of Victoria Poet Laureate; thank you to city and its staff, especially Nichola Reddington. Huge thanks to friend and editor John Barton. Thank you, Vici Johnstone, publisher at Caitlin Press, for believing in my work both as a poet and an editor. Thank you, Sarah Corsie and Malaika Aleba at Caitlin Press for their dedication to books. I thank my students, the Thursday Memoir Group and poetry students from near and far in time and place.

Friends are essential to the work of poets, and I thank The Electronic Garret, The Fiction Bitches and The Waywords. Thanks to Jenna Butler, Ariel Gordon, Anita Lahey, Cynthia Woodman Kerkham, Tanis MacDonald, and Barbara Pelman. Thank you, family: Frodo the dog for keeping me in my chair and for getting me out of it, and Rupert and Colwyn for the love and laughter.

PHOTO BY NANCY YAKIMOSKI

About the Author

Award-winning poet and memoirist Yvonne Blomer is the author of the travel memoir *Sugar Ride: Cycling from Hanoi to Kuala Lumpur,* and four books of poetry, including *As if a Raven* and *The Last Show on Earth.* She works as an editor, teacher and mentor in poetry and memoir, and was the city of Victoria poet laureate from 2015–2018. In 2017 Yvonne edited the anthology *Refugium: Poems for the Pacific* and in 2020, *Sweet Water: Poems for the Watersheds,* both with Caitlin Press. The anthology *Hologram for PK Page,* which Yvonne co-edited, is forthcoming. Yvonne lives, works and raises her family on the traditional territories of the WSÁNEĆ (Saanich), Lkwungen (Songhees), Wyomilth (Esquimalt) peoples of the Coast Salish Nation.